HAITIAN COOKBOOK

MEGA BUNDLE – 2 Manuscripts in 1 – 80+ Haitian - friendly recipes including pancakes, muffins, side dishes and salads for a delicious and tasty diet

TABLE OF CONTENTS

2

Introduction

Haitian recipes for personal enjoyment but also for family enjoyment. You will love them for sure for how easy it is to prepare them.

SIDE DISHES

OLIVE GARDEN ZUPPA TOSCANA

Serves: **6**
Prep Time: **10**   Minutes

Cook Time: **20**   Minutes

Total Time: **30**   Minutes

INGREDIENTS

- 4 turnips
- 3 kale leaves
- 1 onion
- 3 cloves garlic
- ½ bacon slices
- 1,5 L chicken broth
- 250 ml heavy cream
- 1 tsp salt
- 4 tablespoon parmesan
- 1 serving homemade Italian sausage

DIRECTIONS

1. In a pot cook the bacon and transfer bacon aside
2. In the same pot add sausage and cook for 4-5 minutes
3. Add onion, chicken broth, turnings and cook until tender

4. Add kale, heavy cream, salt and stir
5. Add sausage back sprinkle with parmesan and serve

GLUTEN FREE CORN DOGS

Serves: *8*
Prep Time: *10*   Minutes

Cook Time: *30*   Minutes

Total Time: *40*   Minutes

INGREDIENTS

- 2 hot dog sausages

CORN DOG BATTER

- 2 tablespoons almond flour
- ½ tsp xanthan gum
- ½ tsp salt
- ½ tsp baking soda
- ¼ tsp baking powder
- ½ tsp garlic powder
- 1 egg
- 1 tablespoon water

DIRECTIONS

1. In a bowl add all ingredients for the corn dogs and whisk together
2. Dip one sausage at a time and roll the skewer
3. Add the corn dog into hot oil and fry for 30 seconds
4. Serve when ready

Serves: **6**

Prep Time: **10** Minutes

Cook Time: **50** Minutes

Total Time: **60** Minutes

INGREDIENTS

- ½ onion
- ¼ lb. cabbage
- 3 cloves garlic
- 1 tablespoon olive oil
- ¾ lb. ground chicken
- 1.5 lb. ground pork
- 2 tablespoons parsley
- 1 tsp salt
- 1 tsp black pepper
- 1 tsp mustard
- 1 tablespoon Worcestershire sauce
- 3 boiled eggs

DIRECTIONS

1. Preheat oven to 325 F
2. In a frying pan mix all the veggies cook until soft

3. In a bowl mix ground meat, cooked veggies, parsley and spices
4. Add half the meatloaf mixture to a loaf pan and top with boiled eggs
5. Bake for 40-45 minutes, remove and serve

THAI CHICKEN WINGS

Serves: *5*

Prep Time: *10* Minutes

Cook Time: *50* Minutes

Total Time: *60* Minutes

INGREDIENTS

- 2 lb. chicken drumsticks
- 1 lb. chicken wings
- 1 tablespoon olive oil
- 1 tsp salt
- 1 tsp black pepper
- 4 tablespoons thai sweet chili sauce

DIRECTIONS

1. Preheat the oven to 350 F
2. Add the drumsticks and wings to a baking pan and drizzle the olive oil
3. Sprinkle with salt and pepper all over the wings
4. Bake for 40-45 minutes
5. Remove from the oven and transfer to a frying pan, add thai sweet chili sauce

CHICKEN STIR-FRY

Serves: **6**

Prep Time: **10**   Minutes

Cook Time: **20**   Minutes

Total Time: **30**   Minutes

INGREDIENTS

- 5 chicken breasts
- 2 onions
- 2 bell peppers
- 1 cup broccoli florets
- 1 carrot
- 1 clove garlic
- salt
- 1 tablespoon canola oil
- 2 cups brown rice

DIRECTIONS

1. While rice is cooking, sauté chicken the chicken and set aside
2. Sauté onions, garlic, bell pepper, add carrots and broccoli
3. Add chicken back to skillet, season with salt and pepper
4. Serve with brown rice topped with the chicken mixture

HUMMUS

Serves: **4**

Prep Time: **10** Minutes

Cook Time: **20** Minutes

Total Time: **30** Minutes

INGREDIENTS

- 1 can chickpeas
- 1/3 cup water
- 2 tablespoons tahini
- 1 clove garlic
- ½ tsp salt
- 1 tablespoon oil
- 1 tablespoon lemon juice

DIRECTIONS

1. Place all ingredients in a blender and blend until smooth
2. Pour hummus into a container and serve

GRILLED SALMON WITH BASIL

Serves: **4**

Prep Time: **10** Minutes

Cook Time: **20** Minutes

Total Time: **30** Minutes

INGREDIENTS

- 3 salmon steaks
- 2 tablespoons lemon juice
- 2 tablespoons olive oil
- 1 tablespoon basil
- 3 lemon wedges

DIRECTIONS

1. In a bowl mix basil, olive oil, lemon juice and brush both sides of salmon
2. Grill for 10-12 minutes at 150 F
3. Serve with lemon wedges

TUNA MELT

Serves: 2

Prep Time: **10**   Minutes

Cook Time: **10**   Minutes

Total Time: **20**   Minutes

INGREDIENTS

- 1 can tuna
- 1 whole wheat English muffins
- ½ cup canola mayonnaise
- 3 tomato slices
- 1 tablespoon sweet pickle
- 3 slices cheddar cheese
- ½ tablespoon mustard
- 1 tsp tabasco sauce

DIRECTIONS

1. In a bowl mix sweet pickle, tuna, mayonnaise, mustard and tabasco sauce and mix well
2. Spread tuna mixture on each English muffin
3. Top with tomato and cheddar cheese
4. Broil 4-5 minutes until cheese melts

Serves: *2*

Prep Time: *10*   Minutes

Cook Time: *10*   Minutes

Total Time: *20*   Minutes

INGREDIENTS

- 2 whole wheat pita bread rounds
- 2 tomatoes
- 3 tablespoons olive oil
- 3-pieces mozzarella cheese
- 1 garlic clove
- 1 cup basil leaves
- salt

DIRECTIONS

1. Add mozzarella, garlic, basil, tomato and tomato in a bowl and sprinkle with salt, pepper and drizzle with olive oil
2. Place all ingredients in warmed pita pockets

SCRAMBLED EGG SANDWICH

Serves: **2**

Prep Time: **10**   Minutes

Cook Time: **10**   Minutes

Total Time: **20**   Minutes

INGREDIENTS

- 3 slices whole grain bread
- 1 tsp butter
- 1 cloves garlic
- 1 tablespoon dried parsley
- 1 cup egg substitute
- 1 tomato
- ½ tsp salt
- ¼ tsp pepper
- 10 basil leaves
- ½ cup cheddar cheese

DIRECTIONS

1. In a pan melt butter, add garlic, eggs and cook for 2-3 minutes
2. Arrange the egg mixture onto 4 slices of toasted bread
3. Top with basil leaves and sprinkle with cheese

GREEK PIZZA

Serves: **6-8**
Prep Time: **10**   Minutes

Cook Time: **15**   Minutes

Total Time: **25**   Minutes

INGREDIENTS

- 1 pizza crust
- 1 tablespoon olive oil
- 6 oz. spinach
- ¼ cup basil
- 1 tsp oregano
- 1 cup mozzarella cheese
- 1 tomato
- ½ cup feta cheese

DIRECTIONS

1. Spread tomato sauce on the pizza crust
2. Place all the toppings on the pizza crust
3. Bake the pizza at 425 F for 12-15 minutes
4. When ready remove pizza from the oven and serve

CHICKEN PIZZA

Serves: *6-8*

Prep Time: *10*   Minutes

Cook Time: *15*   Minutes

Total Time: *25*   Minutes

INGREDIENTS

- 1 cup cooked chicken breast
- ½ cup bbq sauce
- 1 pizza crust
- 1 tablespoon olive oil
- 1 cup cheese
- 1 cup tomatoes

DIRECTIONS

1. Spread tomato sauce on the pizza crust
2. Place all the toppings on the pizza crust
3. Bake the pizza at 425 F for 12-15 minutes
4. When ready remove pizza from the oven and serve

MARGHERITA PIZZA

Serves: **6-8**
Prep Time: **10** Minutes

Cook Time: **15** Minutes

Total Time: **25** Minutes

INGREDIENTS

- 1 pizza crust
- 1 tablespoon garlic
- 1 tsp salt
- 2-3 tomatoes
- 1 pizza crust
- 4 oz. mozzarella cheese
- 6-8 basil leaves
- ¼ cup parmesan cheese
- ¼ cup feta cheese

DIRECTIONS

1. Spread tomato sauce on the pizza crust
2. Place all the toppings on the pizza crust
3. Bake the pizza at 425 F for 12-15 minutes
4. When ready remove pizza from the oven and serve

EDAMAME FRITATTA

Serves: **2**
Prep Time: **10**   Minutes

Cook Time: **20**   Minutes

Total Time: **30**   Minutes

INGREDIENTS

- 1 cup edamame
- 1 tablespoon olive oil
- ½ red onion
- 2 eggs
- ¼ tsp salt
- 2 oz. cheddar cheese
- 1 garlic clove
- ¼ tsp dill

DIRECTIONS

1. In a bowl whisk eggs with salt and cheese
2. In a frying pan heat olive oil and pour egg mixture
3. Add remaining ingredients and mix well
4. Serve when ready

PICADILLO

Serves: **3**

Prep Time: **10** Minutes

Cook Time: **30** Minutes

Total Time: **40** Minutes

INGREDIENTS

Sofrito
- 2 tbs olive oil
- 5 oz red bell pepper
- 1 oz garlic
- 7 oz onion

Picadillo
- 5 oz potatoes
- 1 oz raisins
- 1 ½ tsp oregano
- 1/3 cup white wine
- 1 tbs tomato paste
- 1 lb beef
- 7 oz tomatoes
- 2 tsp cumin
- 1 tsp cinnamon
- 1 tsp salt
- 3 oz olives
- 2 tbs olive brine

-   2 bay leaves

DIRECTIONS

1.   Sauté the pepper, onions and garlic in oil until tender
2.   Add the oregano, cinnamon, bay leaves and cumin and sauté a little bit more
3.   Add in the beef, tomato paste, wine, potatoes, tomatoes, raisins, and salt
4.   Simmer for about 15 minutes partially covered
5.   Add in the olives and let picadillo cook for about 10 minutes
6.   Stir in the olive brine when finished
7.   Season and serve

CHICKEN STEW

Serves: **2**

Prep Time: **10** minutes

Cook Time: **30** minutes

Total Time: **40** Minutes

INGREDIENTS

- 1/3 cup lime juice
- 1 onion
- 1 ½ cup white wine
- 1/3 cup raisins
- ½ cup oil
- 1 bell pepper
- 1 ½ cup peas
- 1/3 cup orange juice
- 1 lb potatoes
- ¾ cup alcaparrado
- 4 cloves garlic
- 1 can tomato sauce
- Salt
- Pepper
- 1 chicken

DIRECTIONS

1. Mix lime juice, orange juice, chicken, garlic, salt, and pepper

2. Chill for at least 1 hour

3. Cook the marinated chicken for about 10 minutes until browned

4. Cook the pepper and onion until soft, then add wine and cook for another 5 minutes

5. Return the chicken to pan along with the remaining marinade, alcaparrado, tomato sauce, potatoes, ½ cup water, raisins, salt, and pepper.

6. Bring to a boil, then reduce the heat and cook for about 45 minutes

7. Stir in the peas and serve

CHICKEN AND RICE

Serves: **6**

Prep Time: **10**   minutes

Cook Time: **50**   minutes

Total Time: **60**   Minutes

INGREDIENTS

- 3 cloves garlic
- 12 oz diced tomatoes
- 2 tsp cumin
- 3 tsp red pepper flakes
- 4 tbs oil
- 4 cups chicken broth
- 1 tsp saffron
- 3 bay leaves
- 1 tsp salt
- 1/3 tsp black pepper
- 2 ½ lbs chicken
- 2 cups brown rice
- 1 red onion
- 3 bell peppers
- 1 ½ cups green olives
- 3 tbs lime juice

DIRECTIONS

1. Mix the red pepper flakes, lime juice, garlic, salt and pepper
2. Add the chicken and toss to coat
3. Allow to marinate overnight
4. Cook on both sides until golden
5. Warm up the broth and stir in the saffron
6. Saute the onions and peppers until soft.
7. Add in the tomatoes, bay leaves, cumin and rice
8. Cook for about 5 minutes until the juices are absorbed
9. Pour in the broth, add the chicken on top and bring to a boil
10. Reduce the heat and cook covered on low for about 35 minutes
11. Cook uncovered for another 15 minutes
12. Serve topped with cilantro

LOBSTER CREOLE

Serves: *10*

Prep Time: *20* minutes

Cook Time: *40* minutes

Total Time: *60* Minutes

INGREDIENTS

- 6 lobster tails
- 15 oz can crush tomatoes
- 2 lb shrimp
- 1/3 cup olive oil
- 2 onions
- 1 bunch Italian parley
- 1 bay leaf
- 1 cup ketchup
- 2 tsp tabasco
- 1 red pepper
- 5 garlic cloves
- 1 can pimentos
- 2 tbs Worcestershire sauce
- 5 oz tomato sauce
- 1/3 cup wine
- 2 tbs vinegar

- Salt
- Pepper

DIRECTIONS

1. Cut lobster tails into rings and sauté in hot oil until the shells turn red
2. Sauté the onion, garlic, red pepper and bay leaf in the remaining oil for about 10 minutes
3. Stir in the Worcestershire sauce, tomato paste, wine, vinegar, parsley, crushed tomatoes, ketchup, and pimentos
4. Bring to a simmer and cook for 15 minutes, then season with salt and pepper
5. Return the lobster to the pot and simmer for at least 15 minutes
6. Stir in hot sauce
7. Serve immediately

Serves: **8**
Prep Time: **10**   minutes

Cook Time: **60**   minutes

Total Time: **70**   Minutes

INGREDIENTS

- 2 cups rice
- 2 tsp cumin
- 2 tsp fennel
- 1 lb black beans
- 5 cups water
- 1 lb ham
- 3 oregano sprigs
- 3 cloves garlic
- 3 tbs tomato paste
- 1 jalapeno chile
- 3 tbs olive oil
- 2 cups onion
- 2 cups green bell pepper
- 2 ½ tsp salt
- ½ tsp pepper
- 3 bay leaves

DIRECTIONS

1. Rinse the rice and the beans under cold water
2. Place the beans, ham, bay leaves, oregano sprigs, jalapeno and water in a stockpot
3. Bring to a boil, then reduce the heat and simmer for about 40 minutes
4. Pour bean mixture into a colander placed into a bowl, reserving 4 cups liquid
5. Discard jalapenos halves, oregano and bay leaves
6. Remove the ham hock and chop the meat
7. Cook the onion and pepper in hot oil until soft
8. Stir in the cumin, fennel, tomato paste and cook for 5 minutes
9. Add the rice and cook 1 more minute
10. Add ham, black beans, salt, pepper and black beans liquid and bring to a boil
11. Reduce the heat and simmer for 20 minutes
12. Serve immediately

CAULIFLOWER BOWL

Serves: **4**

Prep Time: **10**   minutes

Cook Time: **10**   minutes

Total Time: **20**   Minutes

INGREDIENTS

- 1 sweet potato
- 1 tsp cumin
- 1 tsp oregano
- 4 cloves garlic
- 3 tbs lime juice
- 1/3 cup cilantro
- 5 cups cauliflower florets
- 3 tsp olive oil
- 15 oz black beans
- 1 avocado
- ½ cup pico de gallo
- 3 tsp salt
- 1 tsp black pepper
- 1/3 cup orange juice

DIRECTIONS

1. Mix salt, oil and pepper in a bowl
2. Toss the sweet potatoes in the mixture
3. Roast for at least 10 minutes until tender
4. Mix the lime juice, orange juice, 1 minced garlic clove, 1/3 cup cilantro, oregano, salt, and cumin in a bowl
5. Pulse the cauliflower using a food processor
6. Cook the remaining garlic in hot oil for about half a minute
7. Add the cauliflower, salt, pepper and cook for about 5 minutes
8. Remove from heat and stir in the cilantro
9. Divide among bowls and serve topped with sweet potato, avocado, black beans and pico de gallo

CHICKEN WITH SALSA

Serves: **4**

Prep Time: **15**   Minutes

Cook Time: **15**   Minutes

Total Time: **30**   Minutes

INGREDIENTS
Chicken:
- Pinch chilli flakes
- 1 lb chicken breasts
- 3 tsp garlic granules
- 5 oz grapefruit juice
- 3 tsp cumin
- 2 tsp paprika
- 3 tbs olive oil

Salsa:
- 5 oz grapefruit segments
- 1/3 red onion
- 3 tbs olive oil
- 1 ½ tbs jalapeno pepper
- 3 tbs grapefruit juice
- 2 tbs coriander leaf
- 4 oz jicama

DIRECTIONS

1. Mix the chicken ingredients together except for the chicken breast
2. Place the chicken into the mixture and allow o marinate covered for at least 1 hour
3. Mix the salsa ingredients together in a bowl
4. Cover and refrigerate
5. Grill the chicken for about 5 minutes per side until done
6. Serve with salsa

MEXICAN CHICKEN

Serves: **4**

Prep Time: **10**   Minutes

Cook Time: **20**   Minutes

Total Time: **30**   Minutes

INGREDIENTS

- 2 tsp oil
- 2 chicken breasts
- 2 bell peppers
- 2 cups broccoli florets
- 1 ½ tsp cumin
- 1 tsp cayenne pepper
- 1 tsp paprika

DIRECTIONS

1. Heat a pan
2. Heat the oil for about 20 seconds
3. Add diced chicken and cook for 5 minutes
4. Add the broccoli and peppers and cook for another 10 minutes
5. Add the spices
6. Cook until the water is absorbed

GRILLED SALMON

Serves: **4**

Prep Time: **5** Minutes

Cook Time: **10** Minutes

Total Time: **15** Minutes

INGREDIENTS

- 2 limes juiced
- 1 tbs cilantro
- 1 ½ tsp cumin
- 1 ½ tsp paprika
- 2 lbs salmon
- 1 ½ tbs oil
- 1 tsp onion powder
- 1 tsp chili powder
- 1 avocado
- 2 tsp salt
- 1 red onion

DIRECTIONS

1. Mix the chili powder, onion powder, cumin, paprika, salt and pepper together
2. Rub the salmon with the mix and oil
3. Refrigerate for 30 minutes

4. Preheat the grill
5. Mix the avocado with lime juice, cilantro, and onion together
6. Grill the salmon
7. Serve topped with the avocado salsa

CUBAN QUINOA

Serves: *8*
Prep Time: *15*   Minutes

Cook Time: *4*   Hours

Total Time: *4h 15*   Minutes

INGREDIENTS

- 1 jalapeno
- 2 cups enchilada sauce
- 1 ½ cup chicken broth
- 1 can black beans
- 2 lb butternut squash
- 1 cup corn
- 1 cup quinoa
- 1 tsp garlic
- 1 can tomatoes

DIRECTIONS

1. Peel and deseed the butternut squash
2. Cut into cubes, then place in the slow cooker
3. Add the corn, quinoa, garlic, tomatoes, black beans, jalapeno, enchilada sauce and the chicken broth
4. Give it a good stir, then cook for 4 hours
5. Allow the liquid to absorb while on low for 30 minutes
6. Season with salt and pepper

ROASTED SQUASH

Serves: **3-4**
Prep Time: **10** Minutes

Cook Time: **20** Minutes

Total Time: **30** Minutes

INGREDIENTS

- 2 delicata squashes
- 2 tablespoons olive oil
- 1 tsp curry powder
- 1 tsp salt

DIRECTIONS

1. Preheat the oven to 400 F
2. Cut everything in half lengthwise
3. Toss everything with olive oil and place onto a prepared baking sheet
4. Roast for 18-20 minutes at 400 F or until golden brown
5. When ready remove from the oven and serve

Serves: 2
Prep Time: *10*   Minutes

Cook Time: *20*   Minutes

Total Time: *30*   Minutes

INGREDIENTS

- 1 lb. brussels sprouts
- 1 tablespoon olive oil
- 1 tablespoon parmesan cheese
- 1 tsp garlic powder
- 1 tsp seasoning

DIRECTIONS

1. Preheat the oven to 425 F
2. In a bowl toss everything with olive oil and seasoning
3. Spread everything onto a prepared baking sheet
4. Bake for 8-10 minutes or until crisp
5. When ready remove from the oven and serve

ZUCCHINI CHIPS

Serves: **2**
Prep Time: **10**   Minutes

Cook Time: **20**   Minutes

Total Time: **30**   Minutes

INGREDIENTS

- 1 lb. zucchini
- 1 tablespoon olive oil
- 1 tablespoon parmesan cheese
- 1 tsp garlic powder
- 1 tsp seasoning

DIRECTIONS

1. Preheat the oven to 425 F
2. In a bowl toss everything with olive oil and seasoning
3. Spread everything onto a prepared baking sheet
4. Bake for 8-10 minutes or until crisp
5. When ready remove from the oven and serve

CARROT CHIPS

Serves: *2*
Prep Time: *10*   Minutes

Cook Time: *20*   Minutes

Total Time: *30*   Minutes

INGREDIENTS

- 1 lb. carrot
- 1 tablespoon olive oil
- 1 tablespoon parmesan cheese
- 1 tsp garlic powder
- 1 tsp seasoning

DIRECTIONS

1. Preheat the oven to 425 F
2. In a bowl toss everything with olive oil and seasoning
3. Spread everything onto a prepared baking sheet
4. Bake for 8-10 minutes or until crisp
5. When ready remove from the oven and serve

PASTA

SIMPLE SPAGHETTI

Serves: 2

Prep Time: 5   Minutes

Cook Time: 15   Minutes

Total Time: 20   Minutes

INGREDIENTS

- 10 oz. spaghetti
- 2 eggs
- ½ cup parmesan cheese
- 1 tsp black pepper
- Olive oil
- 1 tsp parsley
- 2 cloves garlic

DIRECTIONS

1. In a pot boil spaghetti (or any other type of pasta), drain and set aside
2. In a bowl whish eggs with parmesan cheese
3. In a skillet heat olive oil, add garlic and cook for 1-2 minutes
4. Pour egg mixture and mix well
5. Add pasta and stir well

6. When ready garnish with parsley and serve

CORN PASTA

Serves: 2

Prep Time: 5   Minutes

Cook Time: 15   Minutes

Total Time: 20   Minutes

INGREDIENTS

- 1 lb. pasta
- 4 oz. cheese
- ¼ sour cream
- 1 onion
- 2 cloves garlic
- 1 tsp cumin
- 2 cups corn kernels
- 1 tsp chili powder
- 1 tablespoon cilantro

DIRECTIONS

1. In a pot boil spaghetti (or any other type of pasta), drain and set aside
2. Place all the ingredients for the sauce in a pot and bring to a simmer
3. Add pasta and mix well
4. When ready garnish with parmesan cheese and serve

ARTICHOKE PASTA

Serves: **2**

Prep Time: **5** Minutes

Cook Time: **15** Minutes

Total Time: **20** Minutes

INGREDIENTS

- ¼ cup olive oil
- 1 jar artichokes
- 2 cloves garlic
- 1 tablespoon thyme leaves
- 1 lb. pasta
- 2 tablespoons butter
- 1. Cup basil
- ½ cup parmesan cheese

DIRECTIONS

1. In a pot boil spaghetti (or any other type of pasta), drain and set aside
2. Place all the ingredients for the sauce in a pot and bring to a simmer
3. Add pasta and mix well
4. When ready garnish with parmesan cheese and serve

SALAD

SLAW

Serves: *1*
Prep Time: 5   Minutes

Cook Time: 5   Minutes

Total Time: *10* Minutes

INGREDIENTS

- 1 cabbage
- 1 bunch of baby carrots
- ½ cucumber
- 1 bun of cilantro
- 1 bunch of basil
- 1 onion

DIRECTIONS

1. In a bowl combine all ingredients together and mix well
2. Serve with dressing

SRIRACHA DRESSING

Serves: *1*
Prep Time: 5   Minutes

Cook Time: 5   Minutes

Total Time: *10*   Minutes

INGREDIENTS

- 1 egg
- ¼ cup rice vinegar
- 1 tablespoon coconut aminos
- 1 tablespoon sriracha
- 1 tablespoon maple syrup

DIRECTIONS

1. In a bowl combine all ingredients together and mix well
2. Serve with dressing

ARUGULA SALAD

Serves: **1**

Prep Time: **5** Minutes

Cook Time: **5** Minutes

Total Time: **10** Minutes

INGREDIENTS

- 2 cups arugula leaves
- ¼ cup cranberries
- ¼ cup honey
- ¼ cup pecans
- 1 cup salad dressing

DIRECTIONS

1. In a bowl combine all ingredients together and mix well
2. Serve with dressing

MASOOR SALAD

Serves: *1*
Prep Time: 5   Minutes
Cook Time: 5   Minutes
Total Time: *10*   Minutes

INGREDIENTS

-   ¼ cup masoor
-   ¼ cup cucumber
-   ½ cup carrot
-   ¼ cup tomatoes
-   ¼ cup onion

SALAD DRESSING

-   ¼ tablespoon olive oil
-   1 tsp lemon juice
-   ¼ tsp green chillies
-   ½ tsp black pepper

DIRECTIONS

1.   In a bowl combine all ingredients together and mix well
2.   Add salad dressing, toss well and serve

Serves: *1*
Prep Time: 5   Minutes

Cook Time: 5   Minutes

Total Time: *10* Minutes

INGREDIENTS

- 1 cup muskmelon
- ½ cup pear cubes
- ½ cup apple cubes
- Salad dressing

DIRECTIONS

1. In a bowl combine all ingredients together and mix well
2. Add salad dressing, toss well and serve

CITRUS WATERMELON SALAD

Serves: **1**

Prep Time: **5**   Minutes

Cook Time: **5**   Minutes

Total Time: **10** Minutes

INGREDIENTS

- 2 cups watermelon
- ¼ cup orange
- ¼ cup sweet lime
- ¼ cup pomegranate

SALAD DRESSING

- 1 tsp olive oil
- 1 tsp lemon juice
- 1 tablespoon parsley

DIRECTIONS

1. In a bowl combine all ingredients together and mix well
2. Add salad dressing, toss well and serve

POTATO SALAD

Serves: *2*
Prep Time: *5*   Minutes

Cook Time: *10*   Minutes

Total Time: *15*   Minutes

INGREDIENTS

- 5 potatoes
- 1 tsp cumin seeds
- 1/3 cup oil
- 2 tsp mustard
- 1 red onion
- 2 cloves garlic
- 1/3 cup lemon juice
- 1 tsp sea salt

DIRECTIONS

1. Steam the potatoes until tender
2. Mix mustard, turmeric powder, lemon juice, cumin seeds, and salt
3. Place the potatoes in a bowl and pour the lemon mixture over
4. Add the chopped onion and minced garlic over
5. Stir to coat and refrigerate covered
6. Add oil and stir before serving

CARROT SALAD

Serves: 2

Prep Time: 5   Minutes

Cook Time: 5   Minutes

Total Time: 10   Minutes

INGREDIENTS

- 1 ½ tbs lemon juice
- 1/3 tsp salt
- ¼ tsp black pepper
- 2 tbs olive oil
- 1/3 lb carrots
- 1 tsp mustard

DIRECTIONS

1. Mix mustard, lemon juice and oil together
2. Peel and shred the carrots in a bowl
3. Stir in the dressing and season with salt and pepper
4. Mix well and allow to chill for at least 30 minutes

MOROCCAN SALAD

Serves: **2**

Prep Time: **5** Minutes

Cook Time: **5** Minutes

Total Time: **10** Minutes

INGREDIENTS

- 2 tbs lemon juice
- 1 tsp cumin
- 1 tsp paprika
- 3 tbs olive oil
- 2 cloves garlic
- 5 carrots
- Salt
- Pepper

DIRECTIONS

1. Peel and slice the carrots
2. Add the carrots in boiled water and simmer for at least 5 minutes
3. Drain and rinse the carrots under cold water
4. Add in a bowl
5. Mix the lemon juice, garlic, cumin, paprika, and olive oil together

6. Pour the mixture over the carrots and toss then season with salt and pepper

7. Serve immediately

AVOCADO CHICKEN SALAD

Serves: **2**
Prep Time: **5**   Minutes

Cook Time: **5**   Minutes

Total Time: **10**   Minutes

INGREDIENTS

- 3 tsp lime juice
- 3 tbs cilantro
- 1 chicken breast
- 1 avocado
- 1/3 cup onion
- 1 apple
- 1 cup celery
- Salt
- Pepper
- Olive oil

DIRECTIONS

1. Dice the chicken breast
2. Season with salt and pepper and cook into a greased skillet until golden
3. Dice the vegetables and place over the chicken in a bowl
4. Mash the avocado and sprinkle in the cilantro

5. Season with salt and pepper and add lime juice
6. Serve drizzled with olive oil

SECOND COOKBOOK

MUSHROOM OMELETTE

Serves: *1*
Prep Time: *5*   Minutes

Cook Time: *10*   Minutes

Total Time: *15*   Minutes

INGREDIENTS

- 2 eggs
- ¼ tsp salt
- ¼ tsp black pepper
- 1 tablespoon olive oil
- ¼ cup cheese
- ¼ tsp basil
- 1 cup mushrooms

DIRECTIONS

1. In a bowl combine all ingredients together and mix well
2. In a skillet heat olive oil and pour the egg mixture
3. Cook for 1-2 minutes per side
4. When ready remove omelette from the skillet and serve

BISCUITS WITH CHEDDAR CHEESE

Serves: **4**

Prep Time: **10** Minutes

Cook Time: **30** Minutes

Total Time: **40** Minutes

INGREDIENTS

- ¼ lb. cheddar cheese
- 2 jalapeno peppers
- ½ lb. almond flour
- 1 tsp baking powder
- ½ tsp baking soda
- ¼ tsp salt
- ¼ tsp paprika powder
- ¼ tsp thyme
- ¼ cayenne powder
- 1 egg
- 1 tablespoon apple cider vinegar
- 5 tablespoons butter
- 4 tablespoons almond milk
- 4 tablespoons sour cream

DIRECTIONS

1. Preheat the oven to 325 F
2. In a bowl add all wet ingredients and mix well
3. In another bowl add all dry ingredients and pour over the wet ingredients and mix well
4. Spoon mixture into a silicone tart mold
5. Bake for 20-25 minutes, remove and serve

MORNING CARROT CAKE

Serves: **12**
Prep Time: **10** Minutes

Cook Time: **35** Minutes

Total Time: **45** Minutes

INGREDIENTS

- **1 recipe cream cheese**
- **1 recipe dairy free whipped frosting**
- **½ lb. carrot**
- **3 eggs**
- **2 oz. coconut oil**
- **4 oz. almond milk**
- **½ lb. almond flour**
- **1 oz. coconut flour**
- **1 tsp stevia powder**
- **½ cup erythritol**
- **1 tsp cinnamon**
- **½ tsp ground cloves**
- **½ tsp cardamom powder**
- **½ tsp allspice**
- **½ tsp baking soda**

DIRECTIONS

1. Preheat the oven to 325 F
2. In a bowl add all wet ingredients and mix well
3. In another bowl add all dry ingredients and pour over the wet ingredients and mix well
4. Pour the carrot cake batter inside your casserole dish
5. Bake for 30-35 minutes, remove and serve

LOW CARB OATMEAL

Serves: **2**
Prep Time: **5**   Minutes

Cook Time: **30**   Minutes

Total Time: **35**   Minutes

INGREDIENTS

- 2 oz. walnuts
- 2 oz. pecans
- 1 oz. sunflower seeds
- 0,7 L unsweetened almond milk
- 3 tablespoons chia seeds
- ¼ tsp stevia powder
- ½ tsp cinnamon

DIRECTIONS

1. **In a blender add walnuts, sunflower seeds, pecans and blend until smooth**
2. **In a pot add the rest of ingredients and blender mixture, simmer for 25-30 minutes on low heat**
3. **When ready, remove and serve**

DAIRY-FREE BREAD

Serves: *6*
Prep Time: *10*   Minutes

Cook Time: *20*   Minutes

Total Time: *30*   Minutes

INGREDIENTS

- 3 egg whites
- 3 egg yolks
- 3 tablespoons mayonnaise
- ½ tsp cream of tartar
- ½ tsp garlic powder
- ¼ tsp parsley

DIRECTIONS

1. Preheat oven to 375 F
2. In a bowl mix cream of tartar and egg whites
3. In another bow mix the rest of the ingredients with a hand mixer
4. Fold the firm meringue into the yolk mixture
5. On a baking sheet add ¼ cup of the foam and spread the mixture
6. Bake for 15-20 minutes
7. Remove and serve

MORNING MUG CAKE

Serves: *1*
Prep Time: *5*   Minutes

Cook Time: *5*   Minutes

Total Time: *10*   Minutes

INGREDIENTS

- 2 tablespoons pumpkin puree
- 2 tablespoons almond utter
- 1 tsp unsalted butter
- 1 egg
- ¼ tsp stevia powder
- ½ tsp baking powder
- ½ tsp cinnamon
- ¼ tsp ground cloves
- ¼ tsp nutmeg
- ¼ tsp ground cardamon

DIRECTIONS

1. In a mug add all ingredients and mix well
2. Microwave for 2-3 minutes
3. Remove, add melted chocolate and serve

CHEESY BISCUITS

Serves: **6**

Prep Time: **10** Minutes

Cook Time: **30** Minutes

Total Time: **40** Minutes

INGREDIENTS

- ¼ lb. shredded gouda
- olive oil spray
- 1 cup almond flour
- 1 tsp baking powder
- ½ tsp baking soda
- ¼ tsp salt
- 1 tsp parsley
- ¼ tsp garlic powder
- 1 tsp rosemary
- ¼ tsp onion powder
- ¼ tsp sour cream
- 1 tablespoon butter
- 1 tablespoon apple cider vinegar
- 2 eggs
- 1 oz. almond milk

DIRECTIONS

1. Preheat oven to 350 F
2. In a bowl add all wet ingredients and mix well
3. In another bowl add all dry ingredients and pour over the wet ingredients and mix well
4. Spoon the mixture into a silicone tart mold
5. Bake for 20-25 minutes
6. Remove and serve

EGG AND VEGGIES BREAKFAST

Serves: **2**

Prep Time: **5** Minutes

Cook Time: **5** Minutes

Total Time: **10** Minutes

INGREDIENTS

- 2 eggs
- 1 tablespoon water
- 1 tablespoon baby spinach
- 1 tablespoon mushrooms
- cherry tomatoes

DIRECTIONS

1. Coat 8 oz. ramekin with cooking spray
2. Add all the ingredients and mix well
3. Microwave for 1-2 minutes
4. Top with tomatoes and serve

SUMMER EGGS

Serves: **1**
Prep Time: **5**   Minutes

Cook Time: **10**   Minutes

Total Time: **15**   Minutes

INGREDIENTS

- 1 tablespoon olive oil
- 1 zucchini
- 6 oz. pack tomatoes
- 1 garlic clove
- 3 eggs
- 4-5 basil leaves

DIRECTIONS

1. In a frying pan add zucchini, fry for 3-4 minutes
2. Add garlic, tomatoes cook for 2-3 minutes and add seasoning
3. Crack in the eggs and cover the pan, cook for 2-3 minutes
4. Top with basil leaves and serve

ALMOND BUTTER CEREAL

Serves: **4**

Prep Time: **10**   Minutes

Cook Time: **30**   Minutes

Total Time: **40**   Minutes

INGREDIENTS

- ½ cup flax seed meal
- ½ cup water
- 1 tablespoon almond butter
- ½ tsp cinnamon
- ¼ raisins

DIRECTIONS

1. Pour boiling water over flax seed meal, stir in cinnamon, almond butter and let it stand for 2-3 minutes
2. Serve with raisins

OVERNIGHT OATS

Serves: *2*
Prep Time: *5*   Minutes

Cook Time: *5*   Minutes

Total Time: *10*   Minutes

INGREDIENTS

- 1 cup Greek yogurt
- ½ cup uncooked oats
- ½ apple
- 8 grapes
- 5 walnuts
- 1 tablespoon almond milk
- 2 drops liquid stevia
- cinnamon

DIRECTIONS

1. In a bowl add all ingredients together and mix well
2. Store in a glass and refrigerate
3. Serve in the morning

AVOCADO TOAST

Serves: **1**

Prep Time: **5** Minutes

Cook Time: **5** Minutes

Total Time: **10** Minutes

INGREDIENTS

- Premade guacamole
- 2 eggs
- 2 slices tomato
- 2 slices gluten-free bread

DIRECTIONS

1. Spread the guacamole over your bread
2. Top with scrambled eggs, salt and tomato slices
3. Serve when ready

BREAKFAST SAUSAGE WITH SWEET POTATO

Serves: **3**
Prep Time: **10**   Minutes

Cook Time: **50**   Minutes

Total Time: **60**   Minutes

INGREDIENTS

- 1 sweet potato
- ½ tablespoon coconut butter
- 3 Applegate naturals chicken
- Apple breakfast sausage

DIRECTIONS

1. Bake sweet potato at 375 F for 45-50 minutes
2. Cook the sausage according to the indications
3. Top the sweet potato with coconut butter and serve

Serves: **4**

Prep Time: **10**   Minutes

Cook Time: **30**   Minutes

Total Time: **40**   Minutes

INGREDIENTS

- ½ CUP whole wheat flour
- ¼ cup boiled green peas
- 1 tsp green chilies
- 1 tablespoon low fat curds
- salt

DIRECTIONS

1. In a blender add green peas and blend until smooth
2. Mix all ingredients with the green peas mixture into a soft dough
3. Divide into 4-6 servings
4. Cook each Paratha in a pan until golden brown
5. Remove and serve

SPORUTS MISAL

Serves: **4**

Prep Time: **10** Minutes

Cook Time: **30** Minutes

Total Time: **40** Minutes

INGREDIENTS

- 2 cups mixed sprouts
- 1 tsp cumin seeds
- 1 tsp chili paste
- ½ tsp cloves powder
- ½ tsp cinnamon powder
- 1 tsp oil
- 1 pinch of salt

DIRECTIONS

1. In a frying pan add cumin seeds, chili paste and cook for 1-2 minutes
2. Add the rest of ingredients and cook for 2-3 minutes
3. Serve the sprouts mixture with onions or tomatoes

Serves: **4**

Prep Time: **10**   Minutes

Cook Time: **30**   Minutes

Total Time: **40**   Minutes

INGREDIENTS

- ½ cup bitter gourd
- 1 cup whole wheat flour
- ½ cup bajra
- ¼ tsp chopped garlic
- ¼ tsp turmeric powder
- 1 tsp chili powder
- 1 tsp coriander
- 1 tsp oil
- salt

DIRECTIONS

1. In a bowl mix all ingredients
2. Divide dough into 8-10 portions
3. Heat a non-stick griddle and cook until golden brown
4. Remove and serve

Serves: *1*
Prep Time: *5*   Minutes

Cook Time: *5*   Minutes

Total Time: *10*   Minutes

INGREDIENTS

- 1 cup Greek yogurt
- ¼ cup oats
- 1 tablespoon almond milk
- 1 tsp chia seeds
- 1 tablespoon honey
- ¼ cup blueberries
- ¼ cup apples

DIRECTIONS

1. In a bowl combine all ingredients together
2. Add honey and mix well
3. Serve when ready

PANCAKES

BANANA PANCAKES

Serves: **4**

Prep Time: **10** Minutes

Cook Time: **20** Minutes

Total Time: **30** Minutes

INGREDIENTS

- 1 cup whole wheat flour
- ¼ tsp baking soda
- ¼ tsp baking powder
- 1 cup mashed banana
- 2 eggs
- 1 cup milk

DIRECTIONS

1. In a bowl combine all ingredients together and mix well
2. In a skillet heat olive oil
3. Pour ¼ of the batter and cook each pancake for 1-2 minutes per side
4. When ready remove from heat and serve

SPROUTS PANCAKES

Serves: **4**

Prep Time: **5**   Minutes

Cook Time: **5**   Minutes

Total Time: **10** Minutes

INGREDIENTS

- 1 cup sprouts
- 1 tablespoon carrot
- ½ cup spinach
- ½ cup fenugreek
- 1 tablespoon besan
- ½ tsp turmeric powder
- ½ tsp cumin seeds
- 1 tsp green chili paste
- 2 tsp soil
- salt

DIRECTIONS

1. In a blender mix sprouts with water and blend until smooth
2. Transfer to a bowl and add he rest of ingredients and mix well
3. Pour mixture into a frying pan and cook for 1-2 minutes per side
4. Repeat with the remaining batter and serve when ready

ZUCCHINI PANCAKE

Serves: 2

Prep Time: 5   Minutes

Cook Time: 5   Minutes

Total Time: 10   Minutes

INGREDIENTS

- ¾ cup zucchini
- ½ cup carrot
- ½ cup rice flour
- ½ cup besan
- 1 tablespoon coriander
- 1 tsp green chilies
- 2 tsp oil
- salt

DIRECTIONS

1. In a bowl mix all ingredients and add ¼ cup water
2. Pour batter into a frying pan and cook for 1-2 minutes per side
3. Repeat with the remaining batter and serve when ready

CHEESE PANCAKES

Serves: *4*

Prep Time: *10*   Minutes

Cook Time: *10*   Minutes

Total Time: *20*   Minutes

INGREDIENTS

- 1 cup almond flour
- ¼ tsp baking soda
- 1 tablespoon brown sugar
- salt
- 3 eggs
- 1 cup cottage cheese
- ¼ cup milk
- 1 tablespoon olive oil

DIRECTIONS

1. In a bowl combine all ingredients together
2. Heat oil in a skillet and pour mixture pancakes
3. Cook each pancake for 1-2 minutes per side
4. When ready remove from the skillet and serve

SIMPLE PANCAKES

Serves: **2**
Prep Time: **5**   Minutes

Cook Time: **5**   Minutes

Total Time: **10** Minutes

INGREDIENTS

- 1 banana
- 2 eggs
- 1 cup milk

DIRECTIONS

1. In a bowl combine all ingredients together
2. Pour mixture into a skillet
3. Cook for 1-2 minutes per side
4. When ready remove to a plate and serve

PEANUT BUTTER SMOOTHIE

Serves: 2

Prep Time: 5   Minutes

Cook Time: 5   Minutes

Total Time: *10*   Minutes

INGREDIENTS

- 1 cup milk
- 1 large banana
- 3 tablespoons peanut butter

DIRECTIONS

1. In a blender place all ingredients and blend until smooth
2. Pour smoothie in a glass and serve

BLUEBERRY & SPINACH SMOOTHIE

Serves: 2
Prep Time: 5   Minutes

Cook Time: 5   Minutes

Total Time: *10* Minutes

INGREDIENTS

- 2 cups spinach leaves
- 1 banana
- 1 cup blueberries
- 1 cup milk

DIRECTIONS

1. In a blender place all ingredients and blend until smooth
2. Pour smoothie in a glass and serve

STRAWBERRY SMOOTHIE

Serves: *1*
Prep Time: *5*   Minutes

Cook Time: *5*   Minutes

Total Time: *10* Minutes

INGREDIENTS

- ¼ orange juice
- 1 cup yogurt
- 1 banana
- 4 strawberries

DIRECTIONS

1. **In a blender place all ingredients and blend until smooth**
2. **Pour smoothie in a glass and serve**

CREAMY BANANA SMOOTHIE

Serves: *1*

Prep Time: *5*   Minutes

Cook Time: *5*   Minutes

Total Time: *10*   Minutes

INGREDIENTS

- 1 cup milk
- ½ cup yogurt
- 1 banana

DIRECTIONS

1. In a blender place all ingredients and blend until smooth
2. Pour smoothie in a glass and serve

AVOCADO SMOOTHIE

Serves: **2**

Prep Time: **5**   Minutes

Cook Time: **5**   Minutes

Total Time: **10**   Minutes

INGREDIENTS

- 1 cup milk
- ½ avocado
- 1 banana

DIRECTIONS

1. In a blender place all ingredients and blend until smooth
2. Pour smoothie in a glass and serve

GREEN SMOOTHIE

Serves: *1*
Prep Time: *5*   Minutes

Cook Time: *5*   Minutes

Total Time: *10*   Minutes

INGREDIENTS

- 1 cup water
- 3 cubes ice
- ½ cucumber
- 2 cups spinach
- 2 cups pineapple

DIRECTIONS

1. In a blender place all ingredients and blend until smooth
2. Pour smoothie in a glass and serve

KIWI SMOOTHIE

Serves: *1*
Prep Time: *5*   Minutes

Cook Time: *5*   Minutes

Total Time: *10* Minutes

INGREDIENTS

- 1 avocado
- 2 kiwis
- ½ cup broccoli
- 1 cup orange juice

DIRECTIONS

1. In a blender place all ingredients and blend until smooth
2. Pour smoothie in a glass and serve

MANGO SMOOTHIE

Serves: *1*
Prep Time: *5*   Minutes

Cook Time: *5*   Minutes

Total Time: *10* Minutes

INGREDIENTS

- 1 cup milk
- 1 cup yogurt
- 1 banana
- 1 cup mango
- 1 teaspoon vanilla extract

DIRECTIONS

1. In a blender place all ingredients and blend until smooth
2. Pour smoothie in a glass and serve

COOKIES

BREAKFAST COOKIES

Serves: **_8-12_**

Prep Time: **5** Minutes

Cook Time: **15** Minutes

Total Time: **20** Minutes

INGREDIENTS

- 1 cup rolled oats
- ¼ cup applesauce
- ½ tsp vanilla extract
- 3 tablespoons chocolate chips
- 2 tablespoons dried fruits
- 1 tsp cinnamon

DIRECTIONS

1. Preheat the oven to 325 F
2. In a bowl combine all ingredients together and mix well
3. Scoop cookies using an ice cream scoop
4. Place cookies onto a prepared baking sheet
5. Place in the oven for 12-15 minutes or until the cookies are done
6. When ready remove from the oven and serve

LOW CARB MORNING COOKIES

Serves: *36*
Prep Time: *15*   Minutes

Cook Time: *15*   Minutes

Total Time: *30*   Minutes

INGREDIENTS

- ½ almond butter
- 1 cup almond flour
- ¼ oat fiber
- ½ tsp salt
- 5 tablespoons powdered erythritol
- ½ tsp stevia powder
- 5 tablespoons chocolate chips
- 1 tablespoon coconut oil

DIRECTIONS

1. Preheat the oven to 325 F
2. In a bowl add almond flour, erythritol, stevia, salt, butter, oat fiber and mix with a stand mixer for a couple of minutes
3. Place the dough on top of a parchment paper and into small pieces using biscuit cutters
4. Bake for 10-15 minutes or until golden brown
5. Remove and dip into chocolate, let it solidify and serve

PUMPKIN CHOCOLATE CHIP COOKIES

Serves: **10**

Prep Time: **10** Minutes

Cook Time: **30** Minutes

Total Time: **40** Minutes

INGREDIENTS

- ½ cup almond butter
- ½ cup pumpkin puree
- ½ cup erythritol
- ½ tsp ginger powder
- ½ tsp nutmeg
- ½ tsp cardamom powder
- ½ tsp cloves
- 1 tsp cinnamon

DIRECTIONS

1. Preheat the oven to 325 F
2. In a bowl mix all ingredients using a hand mixer
3. Place parchment paper oven a baking tray and scoop batter over the baking trays
4. Bake for 20-25 minutes, remove and serve

Serves: **20**
Prep Time: **10**   Minutes

Cook Time: **20**   Minutes

Total Time: **30**   Minutes

INGREDIENTS

- 1 lb. hazelnuts
- 1 tablespoon coconut oil
- 3 tablespoons cocoa powder
- 4 tablespoons powdered erythritol

DIRECTIONS

1. Place the hazelnuts on an oven tray and bake at 300 F for 15-18 minutes
2. Place the hazelnuts in a blender and blend until smooth
3. Add coconut oil and blend for another 10-12 minutes, longer is better
4. Add erythritol, cocoa powder and blend for another 4-5 minutes
5. Remove and serve

BANANA BARS

Serves: **4**

Prep Time: **10** Minutes

Cook Time: **30** Minutes

Total Time: **40** Minutes

INGREDIENTS

- 2 bananas
- 1 tablespoon honey
- 2 tablespoons coconut flour
- 1 cup almond flour
- ½ cup peanut butter
- ½ cup olive oil
- 3 eggs
- ½ tsp salt
- ¼ cup walnuts
- ½ cup raisins
- ½ tsp baking soda

CARAMELIZED TOPPING
- 5 medjool dates
- 1 tablespoon butter
- ½ cup water
- dash salt
- 1 tsp vanilla extract

DIRECTIONS

1. Preheat oven to 325 F
2. In a bowl mix peanut butter, honey, coconut oil, eggs and mix
3. Add coconut flour, salt, baking soda, almond flour and beat well
4. Stir in raisins and walnuts
5. Line a baking dish and spread batter in baking dish
6. Bake for 20 minutes, remove from oven and let it cool
7. In a saucepan add topping ingredients and cook for 12-15 minutes
8. Remove from heat and spread topping over bars

MUFFINS

BREAKFAST MUFFINS

Serves: *8-12*
Prep Time: *10*   Minutes

Cook Time: *20*   Minutes

Total Time: *30*   Minutes

INGREDIENTS

- 8 eggs
- ¼ tsp salt
- 2 onions
- 1 cup ham
- ¼ tsp garlic powder
- ¼ cup mushrooms
- 1 cup cheddar cheese
- ¼ cup spinach

DIRECTIONS

1. In a bowl combine we ingredients and dry ingredients together
2. Fold in mushrooms and mix well
3. Pour mixture into 8-12 prepared muffin cups
4. Bake at 375 for 18-20 minutes
5. When ready remove from the oven and serve

PUMPKIN APPLE MUFFINS

Serves: *8-12*

Prep Time: *10*   Minutes

Cook Time: *25*   Minutes

Total Time: *35*   Minutes

INGREDIENTS

- 2 cups almond flour
- 1 cup brown sugar
- 1 tablespoon pumpkin spice
- 1 tsp baking soda
- 2 eggs
- 1 cup pumpkin puree
- ¼ cup olive oil

DIRECTIONS

1. In a bowl combine dry ingredients and wet ingredients together
2. Add pumpkin puree and mix well
3. Pour mixture into 8-12 muffin cups
4. Cook for 20-25 minutes at 375 F
5. When ready remove from the oven and serve

STRAWBERRY MUFFINS

Serves: **8-12**

Prep Time: **10** Minutes

Cook Time: **25** Minutes

Total Time: **35** Minutes

INGREDIENTS

- ¼ cup olive oil
- ½ cup brown sugar
- 1 egg
- 2 cups almond flour
- 1 tsp baking soda
- ¼ cup almond milk
- ¼ tsp vanilla extract
- 1 cup strawberries

DIRECTIONS

1. In a bowl combine dry ingredients and wet ingredients together
2. Add strawberries and mix well
3. Pour mixture into 8-12 prepared muffin cups
4. Cook for 20-25 minutes at 375 F
5. When ready remove from the oven and serve

ZUCCHINI MUFFINS

Serves: *8-12*
Prep Time: *10*   Minutes

Cook Time: *20*   Minutes

Total Time: *30*   Minutes

INGREDIENTS

- 2 eggs
- 1 cup sugar
- 1 tsp vanilla extract
- 2 cups zucchini
- 2 cups almond flour
- ¼ tsp salt
- ¼ tsp cinnamon
- 1 tsp baking soda
- ¼ tsp baking powder

DIRECTIONS

1. Preheat the oven to 350 F
2. In a bowl combine dry ingredients and wet ingredients together
3. Pour mixture into 8-12 prepare muffin cups and fill 2/3 of the cup
4. Bake for 12-15 minutes
5. When ready remove muffins from the oven and serve

PUMPKIN MUFFINS

Serves: **6**

Prep Time: **5**   Minutes

Cook Time: **20** Minutes

Total Time: **25** Minutes

INGREDIENTS

- 1/3 lb. pumpkin puree
- 1/3 lb. almond butter
- 2 tablespoons coconut oil
- ¾ tsp stevia powder
- ¼ tsp cinnamon
- ½ tsp ground cloves
- ½ tsp cardamom powder
- ½ tsp ginger
- 1 tsp baking powder
- ½ tsp baking soda
- 3 eggs

DIRECTIONS

1. Preheat the oven to 350 F
2. In a bowl mix all ingredients and pour batter into 6 muffin cups
3. Bake for 15-20 minutes, remove and serve

THANK YOU FOR READING THIS BOOK!

CPSIA information can be obtained
at www.ICGtesting.com
Printed in the USA
BVHW031030080321
601999BV00004B/156